By the Hand of Mormon

SCENES FROM THE LAND OF PROMISE

✦ ✦ ✦

By the Hand of Mormon

SCENES FROM THE LAND OF PROMISE

✦ ✦ ✦

Fine Art by Walter Rane

DESERET
BOOK

DESERET BOOK COMPANY
SALT LAKE CITY, UTAH

To my parents, Le Grand and Mildred Rane,

and to my wife, Linda,

and our sons, Peter, Mark, Alex, and Drew.

Thank you.

Quotes on the pages listed below come from the following:

3 (Russell M. Nelson, in *Heroes from the Book of Mormon* [Salt Lake City: Bookcraft, 1995], 3); 6 (Nelson, in *Heroes*, 4); 10 (Nelson, in *Heroes*, 8); 11 (Nelson, in *Heroes*, 15); 14 (John H. Groberg, in *Heroes*, 51); 18–19 (Neal A. Maxwell, in *Heroes*, 66–67); 23 (Cree-L Kofford, in *Heroes*, 71–72); 25 (Kofford, in *Heroes*, 78); 29 (Joseph B. Wirthlin, in *Heroes*, 87); 32 (Wirthlin, in *Heroes*, 93–94); 37 (F. Burton Howard, in *Heroes*, 125); 48 (Mark E. Petersen, "Believers and Doers," *Ensign*, November 1982, 18); 49 (Andrew W. Peterson, in *Heroes*, 160); 52 (Ezra Taft Benson, "The Savior's Visit to America," *Ensign*, May 1987, 4–5); 58–59 (Delbert L. Stapley, "The Savior's Ministry," *Ensign*, May 1974, 102); 62 (Monte J. Brough, in *Heroes*, 193–94); 67 (Gordon B. Hinckley, in *Heroes*, 195–200).

Text © 2003 by Deseret Book

Illustrations © 2003 by Walter Rane

Visit us at deseretbook.com

Library of Congress Cataloging-in-Publication Data

Rane, Walter.
    By the hand of Mormon : scenes from the land of promise / illustrated by Walter Rane.
        p.   cm.
    Includes bibliographical references.
    ISBN 1-57008-919-1 (Hardbound : alk. paper)
    1. Book of Mormon—Devotional literature.   2. Christian life—Mormon authors.   I. Title.
    BX8627.R26 2003
    289.3'22—dc21   2003013410

Printed in the United States of America   42316-7029
Inland Press, Menomonee Falls, WI

10   9   8   7   6   5   4   3   2   1

THAT YE MIGHT BELIEVE ON HIS NAME

That ye might know of the coming of Jesus Christ, the Son of God, the Father of heaven and of earth, the Creator of all things from the beginning; and that ye might know of the signs of his coming, to the intent that ye might believe on his name. HELAMAN 14:12

CONTENTS

PREFACE

When President Ezra Taft Benson called on members of The Church of Jesus Christ of Latter-day Saints to flood the earth with the Book of Mormon, he had something more in mind than simply making copies of the book available throughout the world. "I challenge the homes of Israel to display on their walls great quotations and scenes from the Book of Mormon," he said. "I have a vision of homes alerted, of classes alive, and of pulpits aflame with the spirit of the Book of Mormon messages. . . . I have a vision of artists putting into film, drama, literature, music, and paintings great themes and great characters from the Book of Mormon" ("Flooding the Earth with the Book of Mormon," *Ensign,* November 1988, 5–6).

By the Hand of Mormon: Scenes from the Land of Promise is an answer to President Benson's call. In the pages of this book, you will find dramatic representations of classic scenes from the Book of Mormon: Enos's "mighty prayer and supplication for [his] own soul" (Enos 1:4), Alma's plea for the righteous to "come unto the fold of God" (Mosiah 18:8), Moroni's anguish at being left "alone to write the sad tale of the destruction of [his] people" (Mormon 8:3), and fourteen other moving renditions of Book of Mormon events.

This landmark collection of Book of Mormon paintings, created specifically for this book by award-winning artist Walter Rane, is destined to become known and loved throughout the Church.

The publisher wishes to thank Walter Rane for the remarkable effort, time, and travel that went into each painting and for his willingness to unveil these masterpieces in this format. President Spencer W. Kimball said: "We must recognize that excellence and quality [in art, music, and literature] are a reflection of how we feel about ourselves and about life and about God" ("The Gospel Vision of the Arts," *Ensign,* July 1977, 5). The quality of these paintings is certainly a reflection of how the artist feels about his own life and our loving Heavenly Father.

The publisher also expresses appreciation to Brad Pelo, without whom this project would not have happened; Scott Eggers, who worked many long hours to design the book; and Jana Erickson, Richard Erickson, and Janna DeVore, who helped along the way in a variety of forms.

As you examine the paintings in this book and recall the great stories they represent, it is the publisher's hope that you will be inspired to immerse yourself in the sacred writings that inspired each work of art, that you will help fulfil President Benson's vision "of the whole Church getting nearer to God by abiding by the precepts of the Book of Mormon" ("Flooding the Earth with the Book of Mormon," *Ensign,* November 1988, 6). —THE PUBLISHER

SHE HAD SUPPOSED THAT WE HAD PERISHED

And it came to pass that we took the plates of brass and the servant of Laban, and departed into the wilderness, and journeyed unto the tent of our father. ❖ And it came to pass that after we had come down into the wilderness unto our father, behold, he was filled with joy, and also my mother, Sariah, was exceedingly glad, for she truly had mourned because of us. ❖ For she had supposed that we had perished in the wilderness. **1 NEPHI 4:38, 5:1–2**

A study of Nephi's life provides inspiration as well as information. To me, it is highly significant that his first scriptural statement compliments his parents, Lehi and Sariah (see 1 Nephi 1:1). A sign of greatness then and now is the expression of deferential honor to parents. Lehi and Sariah's family of sons—Laman, Lemuel, Sam, Nephi, Jacob, and Joseph— and unnamed daughters are familiar to readers of the Book of Mormon (see 2 Nephi 5:6). Though Laman and Lemuel often resisted their father's counsel, most of Lehi's children honored him and followed his direction. Foremost among them was Nephi. Nephi's trials in obtaining the plates of Laban are a case in point. —ELDER RUSSELL M. NELSON

THEIR JOY WAS FULL

And it came to pass that after we had come down into the wilderness unto our father, behold, he was filled with joy, and also my mother, Sariah, was exceedingly glad, for she truly had mourned because of us. ❖ And when we had returned to the tent of my father, behold their joy was full, and my mother was comforted. 1 NEPHI 5:1, 7

$\mathcal{A}$lthough the place where Lehi issued the request for his sons
to return to Jerusalem is not known exactly, we do know
that it was along the eastern shore of the Red Sea. The distance
they would have traveled—each way—has been estimated
to be at least 250 miles. That is a long way to go without roads,
cars, cold drinks, or air-conditioning. No wonder Laman
and Lemuel murmured (see 1 Nephi 3:5). No wonder
their mother complained (see 1 Nephi 5:2–3). But Nephi said,
"I will go and do . . ." —ELDER RUSSELL M. NELSON

*T*HE LORD SPAKE UNTO MY
FATHER...AND SAID UNTO HIM:
BLESSED ART THOU LEHI,
BECAUSE OF THE THINGS WHICH
THOU HAST DONE. *1 Nephi 2:1*

THEY DID TREAT ME
WITH MUCH HARSHNESS

We did put forth into the sea and were driven forth before the wind towards the promised land. ❖ And after we had been driven forth before the wind for the space of many days, behold, my brethren and the sons of Ishmael and also their wives began to make themselves merry . . . and to speak with much rudeness, yea, even that they did forget by what power they had been brought thither. . . . ❖ And I, Nephi, began to fear exceedingly lest the Lord should be angry with us, and smite us because of our iniquity, that we should be swallowed up in the depths of the sea; wherefore, I, Nephi, began to speak to them with much soberness; but behold they were angry with me, saying: We will not that our younger brother shall be a ruler over us. ❖ And it came to pass that Laman and Lemuel did take me and bind me with cords, and they did treat me with much harshness. . . . ❖ And it came to pass that after they had bound me insomuch that I could not move, the compass, which had been prepared of the Lord, did cease to work. 1 NEPHI 18:8–12

*T*hroughout Nephi's many activities, he was consistently opposed and threatened, even with death, by Laman and Lemuel. But in each crisis he was miraculously delivered by the power of the Lord and blessed to complete his task. He was a man with

a wide range of human sensitivities, and he yearned for the welfare of those who tormented him. He had a deep love and sense of responsibility for his people, as evidenced by this expression: "But I, Nephi, have written what I have written, and I esteem it as of great worth, and especially unto my people. For I pray continually for them by day, and mine eyes water my pillow by night, because of them; and I cry unto my God in faith, and I know that he will hear my cry." (2 Nephi 33:3.)

Nephi possessed a humility not often seen among gifted men. In fact, he was quite self-deprecating: "Nevertheless, notwithstanding the great goodness of the Lord, in showing me his great and marvelous works, my heart exclaimeth:

O wretched man that I am! Yea, my heart sorroweth because of my flesh; my soul grieveth because of mine iniquities. I am encompassed about, because of the temptations and the sins which do so easily beset me. And when I desire to rejoice, my heart groaneth because of my sins; nevertheless, I know in whom I have trusted." (2 Nephi 4:17–19.)

Though opposed and provoked by them, Nephi did not sever ties with his rebellious brothers until the Lord told him to start a colony of believers. He maintained his affection for them. Rebuke and exhortation were followed by love. We sense . . . some of his sorrow when his brothers rejected the invitation to embrace the gospel of Jesus Christ. —*Elder Russell M. Nelson*

Toward the end of his inspiring life Nephi wrote his concluding testimony and bore witness of the doctrine of Christ, the power of the Holy Ghost, and the truthfulness of the words he had written. Appropriately, his final testimony closed with the words that could be known as his signature: "I must obey." —ELDER RUSSELL M. NELSON

I DID RAISE MY VOICE THAT
IT REACHED THE HEAVENS

Behold, I went to hunt beasts in the forests; and the words which I had often heard my father speak concerning eternal life, and the joy of the saints, sunk deep into my heart. ❧ And my soul hungered; and I kneeled down before my Maker, and I cried unto him in mighty prayer and supplication for mine own soul; and all the day long did I cry unto him; yea, and when the night came I did still raise my voice high that it reached the heavens. ❧ And there came a voice unto me, saying: Enos, thy sins are forgiven thee, and thou shalt be blessed. ❧ And I, Enos, knew that God could not lie; wherefore, my guilt was swept away. ENOS 1:3–6

$\mathcal{E}$NOS KNEW IT WAS IMPORTANT TO PRAY, BUT HE ALSO KNEW IT WAS VITAL TO RECEIVE FORGIVENESS OF HIS SINS AND HE WAS WILLING TO PRAY AS LONG AND AS INTENSELY AS NEEDED AND TO PAY THE PRICE REQUIRED TO ACCOMPLISH THAT WHICH TO HIM WAS VITAL. —*Elder John H. Groberg*

For the multitude being so great that king Benjamin could not teach them all within the walls of the temple, therefore he caused a tower to be erected, that thereby his people might hear the words which he should speak unto them. ⬦ And these are the words which he spake and caused to be written, saying:... ⬦ Behold, I say unto you that because I said unto you that I had spent my days in your service, I do not desire to boast, for I have only been in the service of God. ⬦ And behold I tell you these things that ye may learn wisdom; that ye may learn that when ye are in the service of your fellow beings ye are only in the service of your God. MOSIAH 2:7,9,16—17

*T*he Christocentricity of King Benjamin's ministry and sermon lived on long after him, to say nothing of the influence of Benjamin on millions of us today who are

blessed with his words. He was a model king; but even more important, he was the model of a disciple for all of us. . . .

Nephi, Benjamin's great predecessor, would surely want us to "liken" Benjamin's words unto ourselves (see 1 Nephi 19:23). Such likening would include focusing on quality parenting, which prepares children to overcome the world; making extra efforts to communicate with others, including verifying that they have understood us and we them; valuing the scriptures by searching them; striving for meekness and modesty in our personal lives; putting off the natural man and woman; applying Jesus' great atonement to our own lives; and living so as to merit the regular guidance of the Holy Ghost to keep us in "wisdom's path."

By so doing not only will we enjoy King Benjamin's sermon but we will also apply it. This is what Benjamin would want us to do.

His challenge to his people was to be worthy to "be called the children of Christ, his sons, and his daughters" (Mosiah 5:7). This challenge is the same for us today. How can we live so as to be thus known and deserving of the designation? Benjamin tells us plainly:

"Therefore, I would that ye should be steadfast and immovable, always abounding in good works, that Christ, the Lord God Omnipotent, may seal you his, that you may be brought to heaven, that ye may have everlasting salvation and eternal life, through the wisdom, and power, and justice, and mercy of him who created all things, in heaven and in earth, who is God above all. Amen." (Mosiah 5:15.) *—Elder Neal A. Maxwell*

"HE WAS A MODEL KING; BUT,
EVEN MORE IMPORTANT, HE WAS THE MODEL
OF A DISCIPLE FOR ALL OF US."

And now it came to pass that when Abinadi had finished these sayings, that the king commanded that the priests should take him and cause that he should be put to death. ⬧ But there was one among them whose name was Alma, . . . and he believed the words which Abinadi had spoken, for he knew concerning the iniquity which Abinadi had testified against them; therefore he began to plead with the king that he would not be angry with Abinadi, but suffer that he might depart in peace. ⬧ But the king was more wroth, and caused that Alma should be cast out from among them, and sent his servants after him that they might slay him. ⬧ But he fled from before them. . . . And he being concealed for many days did write all the words which Abinadi had spoken. MOSIAH 17:1–4

*A*nd it came to pass that the king caused that his
guards should surround Abinadi and take him; and they bound
him and cast him into prison. MOSIAH 17:5

Consider the scene…when Abinadi is brought before King Noah and his priests to hear these words: "Abinadi, we have found an accusation against thee, and thou art worthy of death. For thou

hast said that God himself should come down among the children of men; and now, for this cause thou shalt be put to death unless thou wilt recall all the words which thou hast spoken evil concerning me and my people." (Mosiah 16:7–8.)

In all probability, having been in prison, Abinadi has been brought before the king and his priests in some form of physical restraint to minimize the possibility of escape. He has just heard the supreme authority of the land pronounce the death sentence upon him. Without attempting to impart emotions to Abinadi, consider yourself in that same circumstance. Would there not have been a flood of emotion pour over your body? Would there not have been, if only for a moment, a touch of panic, a desire to flee, a hope that the heavens would open and rescue would come? . . . Would you not then have seized upon the words "unless thou wilt recall all the words which thou has spoken evil concerning me and my people" as

the hoped-for route of escape? Would not most of us have sought to find some manner of taking advantage of that opportunity to avoid the sentence of death? Under circumstances such as that, it would not seem too difficult to clothe in respectability the desire to live by simply considering all of the good which you could continue to do if your life were prolonged. . . .

Certainly most of us would be susceptible to some form of thinking along those or similar lines. And now . . . we get a rare glimpse into the heart and mind of Abinadi, for the record states simply: "Now Abinadi said unto him: *I say unto you, I will not recall the words which I have spoken unto you concerning this people, for they are true*" (Mosiah 17:9; emphasis added).

He then underscored with this addendum the faith with which he faced that moment: "I will suffer even until death, and I will not recall my words, and they shall stand as a testimony against you" (Mosiah 17:10). —*Elder Cree-L Kofford*

By the Hand of Mormon

ABINADI'S
GREATEST CONTRIBUTION LIES IN
THE FACT THAT HE LIVED SO AS TO QUALIFY
TO BE THE SEED OF JESUS CHRIST.
HIS LIFE AND DEATH ESTABLISH A
STANDARD BY WHICH WE MIGHT
GAUGE OUR OWN PROGRESS. WHILE IT IS
DOUBTFUL THAT MOST OF US WILL
EVER BE CALLED UPON TO DIE FOR OUR
FAITH IN THE LORD JESUS CHRIST,
IT IS VERY CLEAR THAT EACH DAY WE
WILL BE CALLED UPON TO LIVE FOR
OUR FAITH IN THE LORD JESUS CHRIST.

—Elder Cree-L Kofford

Behold, here are the waters of Mormon . . . and now, as ye are desirous to come into the fold of God, and to be called his people, and are willing to bear one another's burdens, that they may be light; ✦ Yea, and are willing to mourn with those that mourn; yea, and comfort those that stand in need of comfort, and to stand as witnesses of God at all times and in all things, and in all places that ye may be in, even until death, that ye may be redeemed of God, and be numbered with those of the first resurrection, that ye may have eternal life — ✦ . . . if this be the desire of your hearts, what have you against being baptized in the name of the Lord, as a witness before him that ye have entered into a covenant with him, that ye will serve him and keep his commandments, that he may pour out his Spirit more abundantly upon you? MOSIAH 18:8–10

And they were baptized in the waters of Mormon, and were filled with the grace of God. MOSIAH 18:16

Because of Alma's ceaseless labors, the work initiated by Abinadi to redeem the people through faith in the Savior bore good fruits. For over three hundred years, Abinadi's lone convert and his descendants provided spiritual leadership to the Nephite nation.

— *Elder Joseph B. Wirthlin*

And now Alma and those that were with him fell again to the earth, . . . and they knew that there was nothing save the power of God that could shake the earth and cause it to tremble as though it would part asunder. ✦ And now the astonishment of Alma was so great that he became dumb, that he could not open his mouth; yea, and he became weak, even that he could not move his hands; therefore he was taken by those that were with him, and carried helpless, even until he was laid before his father. ✦ And they rehearsed unto his father all that had happened unto them; and his father rejoiced, for he knew that it was the power of God. MOSIAH 27:18–20

Alma the Younger's conversion was brought about by his father's persevering faith. Despite the profound depths of worldly wickedness into which his son had sunk, Alma did not give up on the son he loved. Here is a case where a righteous man surely loathed the sin, but dearly loved the sinner. He diligently, hopefully, fervently prayed for his son. . . . ❖ Alma, upon hearing what had happened to his son and his companions, "rejoiced, for he knew that it was the power of God." Ever the teacher of his people, Alma "caused that a multitude should be gathered together that they might witness what the Lord had done for his son." Alma asked the priests of the Church to come together in fasting and prayer to restore his son's strength, not only for his son's sake but also "that the eyes of the people might be opened to see and know of the goodness and glory of God." (Mosiah 27:20–22.) ❖ When we are faced with the pain of wayward children or of other loved ones who stray from the gospel path, let us remember the persistent faith of Alma. Remember that the prayer of the righteous availeth much (see James 5:16). In fervent, faithful prayers of our own we can seek the Lord's help in reaching out to grasp the hands of loved ones who have lost their grip on the iron rod. —*Elder Joseph B. Wirthlin*

SUCH GREAT FAITH

And [the queen] said unto [Ammon]: . . . ❖ I would that ye should go in and see my husband, for he has been laid upon his bed for the space of two days and two nights; and some say that he is not dead, but others say that he is dead and that he stinketh, and that he ought to be placed in the sepulchre; but as for myself, to me he doth not stink. ❖ Now, this was what Ammon desired, for he knew that king Lamoni was under the power of God. . . . ❖ And he said unto the queen: He is not dead, but he sleepeth in God, and on the morrow he shall rise again; therefore bury him not. ❖ And Ammon said unto her: Believest thou this? And she said unto him: . . . I believe that it shall be according as thou hast said. ❖ And Ammon said unto her: Blessed art thou because of thy exceeding faith; I say unto thee, woman, there has not been such great faith among all the people of the Nephites. ALMA 19:4–6, 8–10

By the Hand of Mormon

MORONI SAID THAT "it was the faith of Ammon and his brethren which wrought so great a miracle among the Lamanites" (Ether 12:15). Missionaries are noted for their faith, and because of Ammon's faith, as well as the faith of many among whom he labored, many miracles accompanied his ministry. The single-handed defeat of the robbers at the waters of Sebus was indeed miraculous. The scripture says that notwithstanding their numbers, Ammon could not be slain (see Alma 18:3). The converting of King Lamoni as a result of spiritual promptings which told Ammon what to do and say was another great miracle. The Spirit bearing witness of the divinity of the Savior to the queen was another. Ammon's rescue of his imprisoned brethren was still another, as was the conversion of thousands of the people of Anti-Nephi-Lehi. Even though the Anti-Nephi-Lehies had committed great iniquity, they were able to take advantage of the redeeming power of the Atonement, they renounced war, and they determined to be perfectly honest and upright in all things and to be firm in the faith of Christ even to the end. This was perhaps one of the greatest of all the miracles. And it was the great faith of Ammon and his brethren, combined with the faith and receptive spirit of the people, that accomplished it. —*Elder F. Burton Howard*

AND IT CAME TO PASS THAT [LAMONI] AROSE,
ACCORDING TO THE WORDS OF AMMON; AND AS HE AROSE,
HE STRETCHED FORTH HIS HAND UNTO
THE WOMAN, AND SAID: BLESSED BE THE NAME OF GOD,
AND BLESSED ART THOU. Alma 19:12

And it came to pass that [Moroni] rent his coat; and he took a piece thereof, and wrote upon it—In memory of our God, our religion, and freedom, and our peace, our wives, and our children—and he fastened it upon the end of a pole. ✦ ... And he took the pole, which had on the end thereof his rent coat, (and he called it the title of liberty) and he bowed himself to the earth, and he prayed mightily unto his God for the blessings of liberty to rest upon his brethren, so long as there should a band of Christians remain to possess the land— ✦ And...he went forth among the people, waving the rent part of his garment in the air, that all might see the writing which he had written upon the rent part, and crying with a loud voice, saying: ✦ Behold, whosoever will maintain this title upon the land, let them come forth in the strength of the Lord, and enter into a covenant that they will maintain their rights, and their religion, that the Lord God may bless them. ALMA 46:12–13, 19–20

He was a man who was firm in the faith of Christ, and he had sworn with an oath to defend his people, his rights, and his country, and his religion, even to the loss of his blood. *Alma 48:13*

But behold, my little band of two thousand and sixty fought most desperately; yea, they were firm before the Lamanites. . . . ✦ Yea, and they did obey and observe to perform every word of command with exactness; yea, and even according to their faith it was done unto them; and I did remember the words which they said unto me that their mothers had taught them. ✦ . . . And to our great astonishment, . . . there was not one soul of them who did perish. . . . ✦ And we do justly ascribe it to the miraculous power of God, because of their exceeding faith in that which they had been taught to believe—that there was a just God, and whosoever did not doubt, that they should be preserved by his marvelous power. ✦ Now this was the faith of these of whom I have spoken; they are young, and their minds are firm, and they do put their trust in God continually. ALMA 57:19, 21, 25—27

NEVER HAD I SEEN so great courage, nay, not amongst all the Nephites. ✦ Now they never had fought, yet they did not fear death; and they did think more upon the liberty of their fathers than they did upon their lives; yea, they had been taught by their mothers, that if they did not doubt, God would deliver them. ✦ And they rehearsed unto me the words of their mothers, saying: We do not doubt our mothers knew it. *Alma 56: 45, 47–48*

HE DID BRING GLAD
TIDINGS TO MY SOUL

I, Samuel, a Lamanite, do speak the words of the Lord which he doth put into my heart; and behold he hath put it into my heart to say unto this people that the sword of justice hangeth over this people; and four hundred years pass not away save the sword of justice falleth upon this people. ❖ Yea, . . . nothing can save this people save it be repentance and faith on the Lord Jesus Christ, who surely shall come into the world, and shall suffer many things and shall be slain for his people. ❖ And behold, an angel of the Lord hath declared it unto me, and he did bring glad tidings to my soul. And behold, I was sent unto you to declare it unto you also, that ye might have glad tidings; but behold ye would not receive me.   HELAMAN 13:5–7

One of the great prophets of ancient times was Samuel

the Lamanite. I like the way he taught.

He was plain and straightforward in his manner

of speech. He did not mince words,

nor did he leave the people wondering what he meant.

—ELDER MARK E. PETERSEN

WHOSOEVER SHALL BELIEVE ON THE SON OF GOD, THE SAME SHALL HAVE EVERLASTING LIFE. . . . THUS HATH THE LORD COMMANDED ME, BY HIS ANGEL, THAT I SHOULD COME AND TELL THIS THING UNTO YOU. *Helaman 14:8-9*

Samuel bravely delivered his message! When denied entrance to Zarahemla he climbed upon the wall of the city. . . . ✦ There are daily walls to climb in our own lives. They present themselves most often as invitations for growth: the daily challenges of parenting, a difficult assignment at work, a new calling in the Church, a sacrament meeting or stake conference talk to present, a lesson to be given in priesthood meeting or Relief Society. —ELDER ANDREW W. PETERSON

And it came to pass that the multitude went forth, and thrust their hands into his side, and did feel the prints of the nails in his hands and in his feet; and this they did do, going forth one by one until they had all gone forth, and did see with their eyes and did feel with their hands, and did know of a surety and did bear record, that it was he, of whom it was written by the prophets, that should come. ✦ And when they had all gone forth and had witnessed for themselves, they did cry out with one accord, saying: ✦ Hosanna! Blessed be the name of the Most High God! And they did fall down at the feet of Jesus, and did worship him. **3 NEPHI 11:15–17**

The record of the Nephite history just prior to the Savior's visit reveals many parallels to our own day as we anticipate the Savior's second coming. ✦ The Nephite civilization had reached great heights. They were prosperous and industrious. They had built

many cities with great highways connecting them. They engaged in shipping and trade. They built temples and palaces.

But, as so often happens, the people rejected the Lord. . . .

There were but few righteous among them (see 3 Nephi 6:14). Nephi led the Church with great power and performed many miracles, yet "there were but few who were converted unto the Lord" (3 Nephi 7:21). The people as a whole rejected the Lord. They stoned the prophets and persecuted those who sought to follow Christ.

And then the God of nature intervened, even Jesus Christ. . . .

For three hours the forces of nature raged. Finally when the thunder, lightning, storm, tempest, and quaking had ceased, a thick darkness settled over the land. For three days no light could be seen, no candle could be lit. The vapor of darkness was so thick that it could be felt, "and there was great mourning and howling and weeping among all the people. . . ." . . .

Then a voice began to speak—a voice from the heavens that was heard throughout the entire land.

The voice spoke of the terrible destruction and announced that this was a direct result of the wickedness and the abominations among the people.

Imagine the feelings of the people when the voice asked, "Will ye not now return unto me, and repent of your sins, and be converted, that I may heal you?" (3 Nephi 9:13).

Then the voice identified itself: "Behold, I am Jesus Christ the Son of God" (3 Nephi 9:15). It was the voice of the very person who had been mocked and ridiculed and rejected by the wicked! It was the voice of Him whom the prophets proclaimed and for whom they were stoned and killed! It was the voice of the Master!

He declared that by Him redemption came, that in Him the law of Moses was fulfilled, and that they were to offer a sacrifice unto Him of a broken heart and a contrite spirit. —*President Ezra Taft Benson*

*F*eel the prints of the nails in my hands and in my feet, that
ye may know that I am the God ... of the whole earth,
and have been slain for the sins of the world. 3 NEPHI 11:14

THEY DID CRY OUT WITH ONE
ACCORD, SAYING: HOSANNA!
BLESSED BE THE NAME OF THE
MOST HIGH GOD! *3 Nephi 11:16–17*

And it came to pass that Jesus spake unto them, and bade them arise. ✦ And they arose from the earth, and he said unto them: Blessed are ye because of your faith. And now behold, my joy is full. ✦ And when he had said these words, he wept, and the multitude bare record of it, and he took their little children, one by one, and blessed them, and prayed unto the Father for them. ✦ And when he had done this he wept again; ✦ And he spake unto the multitude, and said unto them: Behold your little ones. ✦ And as they looked to behold they cast their eyes towards heaven, and they saw the heavens open, and they saw angels descending out of heaven as it were in the midst of fire; and they came down and encircled those little ones about, and they were encircled about with fire. 3 NEPHI 17:19–24

*P*icture yourselves, if you will, among the multitudes to whom Jesus spoke [in America]. . . . Such an outpouring of love they felt for the Savior, and he for them. They shed tears of joy as he

touched their hearts with his comforting words. He likewise felt of their spirit and was filled with compassion and mercy toward them. As he looked over the multitude, he said, "Have ye any that are sick among you? Bring them hither. Have ye any that are lame, or blind, or halt, or maimed, or leprous, or that are withered, or that are deaf, or that are afflicted in any manner? Bring them hither and I will heal them, . . .

" . . . for I see that your faith is sufficient that I should heal you." (3 Nephi 17:7–8.) . . .

Then Christ called the children around him and commanded the multitude to kneel down upon the ground. He likewise knelt and prayed to the Father. The record reads: "And no tongue can speak, neither can there be written by any man, neither can the hearts of men conceive so great and marvelous things as we both saw and heard Jesus speak; and no one can conceive of

the joy which filled our souls at the time we heard him pray for us unto the Father." . . .

Do we feel the sweet spirit of those gathered and the great love Christ expressed to these good faithful people? Here was the great Master Teacher himself giving a lesson in prayer. He was setting the example of being concerned enough about others to pray for them, to pray for their specific and individual needs. He admonished them, "Therefore ye must always pray unto the Father in my name;

"Pray in your families unto the Father, . . . that your wives and your children may be blessed." (3 Nephi 18:19, 21.)

Do we understand what Christ is saying? He is telling us that as he prayed to the Father and healed the sick and blessed the children, that we also have the right to pray for those in need and to bless our own families. This is not only a blessing to us, but a safeguard to family life. —*Elder Delbert L. Stapley*

"Do we understand what Christ is saying? He is
telling us that as he prayed to the Father and healed the sick
and blessed the children, that we also have the right
to pray for those in need and to bless our own families."

Behold, Ether saw the days of Christ, and he spake concerning a New Jerusalem upon this land. ✦ And he spake also concerning the house of Israel, and the Jerusalem from whence Lehi should come—after it should be destroyed it should be built up again, a holy city unto the Lord. . . . ✦ Great and marvelous were the prophecies of Ether; but they esteemed him as naught, and cast him out; and he hid himself in the cavity of a rock by day, and by night he went forth viewing the things which should come upon the people. **ETHER 13:4–5, 13**

*T*he story of Ether was powerful enough to remind Moroni of the eternal nature of hope. Hope is both a predecessor and a derivative of faith. One may not be able to know or testify

about things which are not seen, but one surely can have strong and significant hope. Neither Moroni nor Ether despaired or were much discouraged about the conditions and consequences of their lives. Each was given a deep and abiding faith in the mission of the Lord Jesus Christ. The following is what Ether's words inspired Moroni to say about hope, which must precede and grow into "a more excellent hope:" "And I also remember that thou hast said that thou hast prepared a house for man, yea, even among the mansions of thy Father, in which man might have a more excellent hope; wherefore man must hope, or he cannot receive an inheritance in the place which thou hast prepared" (Ether 12:32).

In facing tragedy, it is instructional to observe those who have complete and total faith in the reality of the mansions of our Father. This faith does result in a testimony of Jesus Christ and the process of the Atonement. "Man must hope, or he cannot receive" the blessing of the great plan of happiness, which provides peace and understanding for mortal mankind. It is this "more excellent hope" that allows us to accept whatever trial or test comes to us.

As each of us faces personal tragedy, we can have a much better acceptance of the final results because of the prophet Ether's example. Even the last words written and recorded by Ether are instructional and helpful in our personal lives. One can feel the great accord and peace which was manifest during his final mortal days: "Now the last words which are written by Ether are these: Whether the Lord will that I be translated, or that I suffer the will of the Lord in the flesh, it mattereth not, if it so be that I am saved in the kingdom of God. Amen." (Ether 15:34.) —*Elder Monte J. Brough*

Now the last words which are written by
Ether are these: Whether the Lord
will that I be translated, or that I suffer
the will of the Lord in the flesh,
it mattereth not, if it so be that I am saved
in the kingdom of God. Amen. *Ether 15:34*

Behold I, Moroni, do finish the record of my father, Mormon. Behold, I have but few things to write, which things I have been commanded by my father. ❖ And now it came to pass that after the great and tremendous battle at Cumorah, behold, the Nephites who had escaped into the country southward were hunted by the Lamanites, until they were all destroyed. ❖ And my father also was killed by them, and I even remain alone to write the sad tale of the destruction of my people. But behold, they are gone, and I fulfil the commandment of my father. And whether they will slay me, I know not. MORMON 8:1–3

By the Hand of Mormon

*O*f all the characters who walk the pages of the Book of Mormon, none stands a greater hero, save Jesus only, than does Moroni, son of Mormon. ✦ He was skilled as the commander of an army of ten thousand warriors. He was concise as an editor and historian. He was prophetic in speaking of his own and future generations. He was a man who walked alone for years, a fugitive from his enemies who were unrelenting in their pursuit. Moroni was military commander, prophet-historian, the last of the Nephite survivors. . . .

While wandering as a lonely fugitive, Moroni added to his father's record. His words ring with pathos: "I would write . . . if I had room upon the plates, but I have not; and ore I have none, for I am alone. My father hath been slain in battle, and all my kinsfolk, and I have not friends nor whither to go. . . . And behold, the Lamanites have hunted my people, the Nephites, down from city to city and from place to place, even until they are no more. . . . " (Mormon 8:5, 7.)

Who can sense the depth of his pain, the poignant loneliness that constantly overshadowed him as he moved about, a fugitive relentlessly hunted by his enemies? For how long he actually was alone we do not know, but the record would indicate that it was for a considerable period. His conversation was prayer to the Lord. His companion was the Holy Spirit. There were occasions when the Three Nephites ministered to him. But with all of this, there is an element of terrible tragedy in the life of this man who became a lonely wanderer. . . .

He wrote his last testament in the book which carries his name and which concludes the Nephite record. He wrote as one with a certain knowledge that his record would eventually come to light. He expressed the hope that perhaps a few more things might be of worth unto his brethren the Lamanites, in some future day (see Moroni 1:4). . . .

That translated record, the Book of Mormon, is here today, available for all to handle. It has come as a voice speaking from the earth in testimony of the divinity of the Lord Jesus Christ. It goes hand in hand with the Bible as another witness of the Redeemer of the world.

Terrible was Moroni's ordeal in life as he witnessed the decay of his civilization and the total destruction of his people. Terrible was his loneliness as he wandered, a fugitive, the last of his race. Glorious has been his return to earth as a resurrected being, a testament to this and succeeding generations of the truths of the ancient record, and of its validity for us and all people as another witness of the Lord Jesus Christ. —*President Gordon B. Hinckley*

This book and the musical album by the same name represent a collaboration designed to honor the messages and people of the Book of Mormon, a book that invites each of us to come unto Christ. ✦ Though the paintings in this book and the musical story told on the CD are intentionally not integrated, it is hoped that each will be magnified by the presence of the other. Both the art and the music are intended to increase appreciation for the Book of Mormon and help fulfil President Ezra Taft Benson's vision of "artists putting into . . . music and paintings great themes and great characters from the Book of Mormon" ("Flooding the Earth with the Book of Mormon," *Ensign,* November 1988, 6).

THE ART Walter Rane's seventeen original oil paintings (which measure on average 40 by 50 inches) capture the essence of the message behind a number of classic Book of Mormon events—from Nephi and his brothers returning with the plates of brass to Captain Moroni raising the title of liberty to the great prophet Moroni mourning the loss of his father, Mormon.

To create this collection, Walter carefully researched what is known about the early inhabitants of the Americas and even took a ten-day trip to Central America with David Pliler to help compile sketches and background material for the completion of his work. While it was his intent to be consistent with what scholars know about the locations and lifestyles of the Book of Mormon, he recognizes that there is still much that remains unknown.

Walter Rane—Artist. Walter Rane, whose renditions of scriptural text have elicited comparisons to master painters such as Rembrandt, studied at the Art Center College of Design in Los Angeles, California. His studies included classes on anatomy and classical drawing, something many schools during the early 1970s weren't teaching. As such, his paintings demonstrate a high degree of anatomical accuracy and color mastery.

After college, Walter began his career in New York City as a freelance book and magazine illustrator. In 1994, after more than twenty years of commercial work, he moved his family to Oregon to focus on portraiture, landscapes, and the scriptural studies for which he is becoming well known among Latter-day Saints. Shortly after his move to Oregon, The Church of Jesus Christ of Latter-day Saints commissioned Walter to do a mural for its visitors' center at Winter Quarters, Nebraska. The project sparked his interest in religious painting, and he has continued to work on such efforts as the Book of Mormon paintings in this book, a representation of the Last Supper, and a striking piece of Christ healing a blind man.

In 2002, Walter and his family returned to New York City, where he worked exclusively on this collection.

THE MUSIC Sam Cardon, who originally envisioned this project, has created music based on a story by David Pliler. The story follows the life of Mormon from his boyhood calling by Ammaron the prophet to the final battle at Cumorah's Hill. The story is written for performance as a musical stage-play, but the songs on the album have universal themes that will inspire the listener and create anticipation for live performances.

Sam Cardon—Composer. Sam Cardon is an Emmy Award–winning composer whose credits include twenty-four film scores. He provided three hours of original music for the 1988 Winter Olympic Games in Calgary and recently provided music for closing ceremonies at the 2002 Salt Lake City Olympic Winter Games. Sam's religiously themed work includes arrangements for the Mormon Tabernacle Choir and the LDS Church's production, *Light of the World.* He also collaborated on the musical scores for the PBS documentaries *Trail of Hope* and *American Prophet.*

David Pliler—Playwright and Lyricist. David Pliler obtained a BFA from Brigham Young University and a master's degree in screenwriting from the University of California—Los Angeles. David is a member of the Screen Actors Guild and has appeared in television and film, including commercials for the Church. David and his family reside in southern California, where he is a freelance writer.

Like others who have undertaken artistic expression in an attempt to bring glory to God, the creators of this book and the separate musical CD realize that our measure is small and that any real contribution in our craft comes only when we allow His Spirit to magnify us. The result is a gift we have at last received and not one we have actually given.

Walter Rane

Sam Cardon

David Pliler